"Charltonian"

A Family Bus Bu   **ınd**
Ironstone D

GW00385574

Joh
and Philip Battersby

Table of Contents

1. Introduction

The name "Charltonian" was used by my grandfather John Dobson, who ran buses at Charltons village near Guisborough until 1930. In the exploration of my family's history it occurred to me to seek the help of bus enthusiasts in the hopes of learning something about my grandfather's business activities. The putting together of the family history and the known details of the buses and bus services creates a fascinating story of interest well beyond the confines of the family, adding significantly to local and industrial recorded history. I have been assisted by Philip Battersby, whose researches and compilation have enabled me to tell the tale thoroughly. I hope you like it.

2. An Ironstone Mining District

In the nineteenth century the Cleveland area of Yorkshire was extensively mined for ironstone which was taken by rail to various furnaces, principally in the Middlesbrough area. Today if you take the main Whitby road out of

---

*Title page photographs: [1] John Dobson, 1867 - 1945. [2] Guisborough is the local market town and had a population of about 7,000 until its huge expansion as a dormitory town for industrial Teesside in the 1960s. In a view of Westgate and Market Place in the late 1920s, the small bus was probably **PY 5202** making its way to Lingdale. The name "Charltonian Bus Service" is just about decipherable on the original, and the distinctive deeply domed roof compares directly with what can be seen in the views on page 17. St Nicholas parish church keeps a benevolent eye on the proceedings, and the dramatic abbey ruins are just out of sight to the right. (Picture postcard)*

An ironstone mining village: these two views of Charltons perhaps date from Edwardian times (top) and the 1930s. They set the scene for the development of the Charltonian Bus Service. The third row of houses (on the right in each picture) has since been demolished. (Freddie Dadd and June Henderson Collections)

This remarkable view eastward across the valley to Birk Brow shows Margrove Park cottages and the mineral railway and spoil tips. (Freddie Dadd Collection)

Guisborough, in about a mile and a half you come (on your right) to the site of Spawood mine, now prominent as a motor scrapyard. In the next half-mile the trackbed of the railway line, which until 1958 carried a Middlesbrough-Whitby passenger service via the coast, runs alongside the road and includes a substantial viaduct, disused since 1964 and now screened by trees from the motorist's view. The road then used to cross the railway by a narrow skew bridge at Slapewath ('Fox and Hounds') where there was another mine (Spa), the workings of which were largely underneath the railway.

As you continue along the road, with the railway trackbed now on your left (i.e. to the north) you come in another 400 yards to Charltons village which is on your right and is nowadays by-passed. This former mining settlement consists of two long rows of houses, originally numbers 1 to 95 on the front and 2 to 96 at the back, and there was formerly a rather shorter third

row behind the second. This third row was demolished in 1953 because of mining subsidence. Modern road improvements have left sections of the old main road largely undisturbed both at Slapewath and at Charltons.

A third mine, Slapewath, was established by Thomas Charlton and Company in 1864, and was reached by a mineral branch line which left the main railway at Slapewath village and passed under the road to the mine's drift entrance. It was here that Charltons village was subsequently built to house the miners, who lived almost on the job. In those days without local public transport there could be little alternative. Up in the hills some distance to the south, shafts were sunk in 1878 and 1880 to replace the drift entrance in the hillside.

Half a mile up the lane towards Boosbeck you come to Margrove Park - 'Magra' in local parlance - which is another former mining settlement. Nowadays Margrove Park boasts a

4

Above: The earliest picture of John Dobson shows him with this laden cart.

Below: The smart cab with John Dobson holding the reins needed only one horse, but it moved during the exposure of the photograph to create an impression of two horses with at least six ears! (Both: Dobson Collection)

JOHN DOBSON, Hearse, Cab and Brake Proprietor.

Weddings, Funerals, and Pleasure Parties accommodated at reasonable prices

ALL ORDERS PROMPTLY ATTENDED TO.

Note the Address:— **94, Charlton's Terrace, Slapewath, near Guisbro'.**

The two-horse brake was standing opposite the Fox & Hounds at Slapewath about 1900 - it is still a local landmark although now a different building. (Freddie Dadd Collection)

highly regarded Heritage Centre which, in conjunction with the Tom Leonard Mining Museum at Skinningrove, keeps alive the industrial memory of the district. The booklet *Cleveland Ironstone* by S Keith Chapman (32 pages, Dalesman Books, 1973, ISBN 0 85206 181 1) gives a brief introduction to the mining of ironstone in the district, principally in the 19th century but not finally ceasing until 1964. Surviving remnants of this once extensive industry are now few, with other industrial usage, afforestation, housing developments, road improvements, off-road motor cycling, gradual decay and vandalism combining to change the landscape as drastically as the mining industry itself did some 150 years ago.

3. John Dobson

John Dobson was born in Westerdale in 1867, the son of an itinerant farm labourer, although earlier generations were farmers in Moorsholm and earlier still they were at Mickleby, where we can be traced back to the 17th century. When he was 14 the 1881 census described John as an indoor farm servant in the household of Thomas Shaw in Commondale, probably because he was born with a deformed leg which never grew from the age of seven. Family folklore has it that he had a hay fork stuck through his foot and it never grew after that incident. Despite this, when he was 24 the 1891 census recorded that he was an ironstone miner and lived at Charltons.

4. The Edwardian Years - 1901 to 1910

By the time he was 34 the 1901 census listed John Dobson as a hearse, brake and cab proprietor, and he occupied premises at the western end of Charltons village, i. e. towards Slapewath. The vehicles were of course horse-drawn, and the earliest surviving picture of John Dobson shows him driving a small cart loaded with heavy sacks. A typical advertisement of the period, placed in the Methodist magazine for the Cleveland East area in 1902, includes a picture of John Dobson in charge of a cab. One of the brakes is illustrated in a photograph at the Fox and Hounds public house at Slapewath, although the building shown here has long been replaced by the present one on the same site.

Two brakes can be seen in a fourth photograph, said to have been taken in 1901, which shows John Dobson on the right with his daughter Annie, who looks to have been aged about 3 or 4. In her old age as Mrs Annie Nunn she contributed this picture and some memories to the Evening Gazette, and they were published on Saturday 16th June 1973. She was then aged 75 and still lived at Margrove Park. Also in the 1901 picture are John's wife Sarah, his brother George, and (at far left) Ethel Craig, a friend of the family. The most prominent of the vehicles was "The Mayflower", pride of the fleet.

Mrs Nunn gave a vivid picture of her memories of the early days of the century. "Those were the days of the horse brakes which father ran from Charltons to Guisborough and further afield. He used to get up at 5am to take people to Guisborough station, and often be there at night to meet the 11pm train back. When a man or boy was injured in the local mines, he used a conveyance to take the patient to the

Above: John Dobson and his young daughter Annie and other family members were photographed at the depot and stables at Charltons circa 1901.

Below: The new motor car: John Dobson with his wife Sarah and some of the family pose outside the house with their dramatic acquisition, the De Dion car *AJ 443*. It was not for fun in such hard times, and had to earn its keep and more. The three small boys are his sons Albert, Bill and Walter, and the man standing next to the car is his brother George. (Both: Dobson Collection)

Admiral Chaloner Hospital in Guisborough. He also catered for weddings, and for funerals for which he had a hearse and cabs. He was also a coalman, delivering at 10d a hundredweight, and had a milk delivery service which operated twice a day, with fresh milk 2d a pint. On Saturday afternoons in the winter months the local football teams travelled to away matches in the horse brakes, and in summer the cricket teams used the same means of getting there and back. When the conveyance had to descend a hill, Mr Dobson, or a helper, sat in a special seat at the rear and operated a wheel which applied the brakes. Often on steep hills the passengers had to get out and walk to ease the work of the horses. We had brakes running to Redcar for the races on Whit Monday, and down to the seaside with families out for the day. In fact the only time off came on Good Friday (when, if the weather was fine, all the men planted early potatoes in their gardens), Christmas Day and New Year's Day. Happy days!"

5. The Motor Car - circa 1909 to 1920

It was a great event when John Dobson acquired an 8hp De Dion Bouton motor car which had been owned by Dr W W Stainthorpe, of Guisborough. According to family folklore this was "the first taxi in Cleveland" and given John's disability, it is clear that cab driving was an occupation which he could follow. He was taught to drive by John Close, who was Dr Stainthorpe's chauffeur. The car was registered AJ 443 and is illustrated with John at the wheel outside the end house at Charltons, which was No. 96. As their address was shown as No. 94 in the advertisement, they probably had two houses together (94 and 96) - there were 12 in the family at that time. Sarah and some of the children made sure not to miss being in the picture. There is some doubt about the date of the acquisition of AJ 443, thought to be by 1909, but described as 1911 by Mrs Nunn. Just outside Charltons on the Guisborough road and adjacent to the aforementioned surviving viaduct is Fancy Bank. This was very steep before road improvements in 1948, as is shown by observing the original bridge which has been restored. Many stories tell of trips when the poor De Dion had to be reversed up the bank because reverse was lower than any of the forward gears.

Motor tax records give better information about another motor vehicle, which could either have augmented or replaced the De Dion. The newcomer was a Napier charabanc which had been registered DC 337 on 20th June 1912. There is no record of its seating capacity, and it could have been quite small, say an 8-seater. It was a year old when purchased by John Dobson on 30th June 1913 - at least, that is the date when the change of owner was recorded. There is nothing to indicate whether Dobson used this on a regular service, and at least as regards Middlesbrough Council, no hackney carriage licence appears ever to have been issued by them for this vehicle. It passed to a third owner, as a lorry, the transfer being recorded on 1st September 1920.

Alf Armstrong of Guisborough tells the story of the Guisborough church trip to Scarborough in the new fangled mode of transport in which his mother

Daisy was a passenger. On the day in question the charabanc didn't turn up. The entire group then walked to Charltons, where the chara was jacked up having new wheel bearings fitted. The trip itself was not without incident. "We were going up Birk Brow when the radiator started to boil and everybody was sprayed with steam. We were only going slowly so everybody jumped off when I shouted that I thought it was going to blow up". It went without saying that on the return trip via Sandsend, everyone had to walk up Lythe bank.

6. More about the Family

John Dobson had three sons. Albert the eldest was both mechanic and driver, Bill (my father) was a driver and Walter came into the business straight from school as a conductor. My father is clearly shown at the wheel of a solid-tyred charabanc in the lower picture opposite, taken at Scarborough railway station. There were two Dobson girls, Annie and Jinny, who married the two brothers Wilf and Alf Smith who also were drivers for Charltonian. In later life Annie had remarried and was the Mrs Nunn whose memories compiled in 1973 are quoted above.

7. The Beginnings of Bus Operation - 1921

The next vehicle known to have been acquired by John Dobson was a 14-seat Ford convertible registered DC 1109, and likely to have been purchased new in 1920. This probably replaced the Napier charabanc DC 337 sold in September of that year. There is no particular evidence of how his traffic developed in the immediate locality but the idea, ambitious at that date, to run a bus service from Lingdale into Middlesbrough surfaced in 1921, when Dobson was already 54. On 28th May he applied to Middlesbrough Council to operate such a service with the Ford convertible DC 1109, and on 19th July made a second application, this time for DC 1189 [1], also a Ford convertible. Temporary licences were granted.

In addition, Lewis Brechner and Angelo Rea were at this time both

>> *Opposite page: An outing in a Charltonian charabanc with a more modern 'torpedo' style of body seating 14 but still on solid tyres was photographed at Scarborough with Bill Dobson at the wheel. The registration number is not visible, but the wheels and what might be a V-shaped radiator are distinctive. They are thought to identify the Maxwell AJ 4610. If so, the year is probably 1924 - that vehicle was with previous owner Robinson's in 1923, and was licensed as a bus rather than a charabanc in January 1925. (Freddie Dadd Collection/Courtesy Kirkleatham Museum)*

[1] - It seems rather unlikely that John Dobson would have been able to acquire two Ford convertibles at about the same time and obtain two temporary licences on different dates. What seems more probable is that he had one such vehicle, which was licensed for a month and for which he then applied to renew. The second temporary issue (on 19th July 1921) is not recorded in the Minutes of the time and is known only from a later reference in 1924. Transcription errors in the Council Minutes are not unknown and tend to be perpetuated in later references, and there is a fair probability that in this case one of DC 1109 or DC 1189 is an error for the other.

Above: The original of this picture was found among his mother's effects by Freddie Dadd, and a note on the reverse tells us that it shows one of John Dobson's charas taking the staff of the Co-op store on a day trip to Scarborough. The location of the John Smith's pub (Tadcaster Ales) with G Wiltshire as landlord is unnamed. The Thornycroft chassis identified by the unusual wheels appears to have been registered in County Durham as *J 2611* (in 1914) although the single letter is partly obscured.

running on this route, and none of the three ran to a timetable. In the case of DC 1109 Dobson's licence was granted on 21st June, and the Minutes recorded that this was for pleasure parties only (what we would now call private hire), and was not to be deemed to authorise establishment of a regular route. There seemed to be a grey area in which operation 'as required', rather than to a published timetable, was interpreted (at least by the operators) as being within the terms of the licences. In the event, Dobson's licence(s) expired on 11th October 1921 and his service was discontinued. This was not before the licensing committee had noted (on 9th September) that the vehicles of several operators including John Dobson were not suitable for route work during wet weather. 'Route work' would appear to mean what we would now call a bus service as distinct from an excursion or private hire, and a 'convertible' had a variable lorry, van or bus body with canvas roof or sides for wet weather, as illustrated opposite.

8. An Uncertain Period - 1921 to 1924

With the fizzling out of the Lingdale-Middlesbrough bus service in what was everywhere a difficult economic year, it seems that John Dobson's business made little progress in the period that followed. There was no further reference to him in Middlesbrough until 1924. In particular, a list for annual bus licence renewals in September 1923 did not include any known Dobson vehicle.

A spur was provided by Jones and Ransome's Cleveland Bus Service, when they commenced a Lingdale-Middlesbrough route on 8th March

1924. John Dobson made an application for a similar service on 20th May, but in view of his previous operations in 1921, the committee now wanted to know whether he proposed a regular daily service or just to run as required. On 17th September the decision was put in the hands of the Town Clerk and Hackney Carriage Inspector, and they quickly granted the application and Dobson commenced his service.

There is no immediate record of what bus Dobson might have used on this service, given that his Ford convertible(s) were already considered unsuitable in 1921. The most likely candidate is the Albion X 7953 which features in a well-known photograph taken in Queen's Square, Middlesbrough for W G Edmond the local coachbuilder. The conductor on the step is Reg Handley of Charltons. The Northumberland registration number of the bus dates from 1919 but the enclosed saloon body, probably a 14-seater, is of a style that Edmond was producing from 1923. The most particular feature is the solid tyres - 1923 was really the last year that an operator could get away with these tyres on so small a bus. The giant pneumatic tyre was rapidly becoming a reliable proposition, and in 1923 United Automobile Services was fitting these to a substantial number of 26-seat Daimlers, the largest buses then capable of using them satisfactorily.

9. Middlesbrough to Lingdale, 1925 to 1927

Following the initial granting of a licence in September 1924, John Dobson's bus service between Lingdale

*The above style of bus body was produced by Edmond for quite a lengthy period from 1923, despite rapid change throughout the industry in those years. Dobson's **X 7953** in Queen's Square, Middlesbrough, was perhaps the first example of the type. Also in 1923 was the ubiquitous Ford T (below) with convertible van/bus body incorporating canvas sides with windows. This one for T H Southall was registered **PT 1410** and had early pneumatic tyres; it was later Dobson's. (Both: Edmond & Milburn Ltd)*

and Middlesbrough settled down and developed. Middlesbrough Council's excellent records afford us much valuable information and enable us to build up quite a comprehensive picture, although it is always from the Middlesbrough point of view. The service, and each individual vehicle, had to be licensed, and the licences were always for specific periods and therefore had to be renewed, usually annually. An operator had to sign his acceptance of the terms and conditions of his licence, and an example of the declaration is reproduced here. It is dated 10th February 1925 and confirms that the route into Middlesbrough was via Ormesby Road, with the terminus outside the Post Office. This was adjacent to the Exchange where a bus station would subsequently be built, and the GPO building now

HACKNEY CARRIAGE DEPARTMENT,

CENTRAL FIRE STATION,

MUNICIPAL BUILDINGS,

MIDDLESBROUGH.

10th February. 1925.

In consideration of the County Borough of Middlesbrough Hackney Carriage Committee granting me licenses for Motor Omnibuses, I agree to the following terms and conditions, viz : -

To ply for hire between Middlesbrough and Lingdale, via, Ormesby Road, Westbourne Grove, West Terrace, North Ormesby Road, Marton Road to the Post Office, subject to an undertaking not to pick up passengers in the Borough whose destination is within the Borough or to run in competition with the Tramways or Motor Omnibuses of the Corporation or the Cars of the Tees-side Railless Traction Board.

2. That the Omnibuses shall run in a regular service according to a time-table to be approved by the Hackney Carriage Inspector of the Corporation.

3. That in respect of all return tickets issued on this service arrange-ments will be made for the persons taking such tickets to be returned to the place in respect of which the payment has been made and on the last return journey sufficient accommodation to be left available to carry return passengers. If for any reason the number of outstanding return passengers exceeds the capacity of the omnibus, arrangements to be made for a further journey, in order to pick up any passengers that may be so left.

4. That the fares charged shall be subject to the approval of the Hackney Carriage Inspector of the Corporation and shall be exhibited in the Omnibuses.

5. That the condition of the Omnibuses and the route traversed within the Borough be subject to the approval of the Hackney Carriage Inspector at all times.

John Dobson's acceptance of licence and conditions, 10th February 1925. (Courtesy Teesside Archives)

Signed. *John Dobson*

96 Charlton,

BOOSBECK, S.O.

14

appropriately houses the Teesside Archives, including the original of this signed acceptance. Most of the wording follows a standard form, and it is clear that problems had been experienced with operators running several journeys into town, with most of the passengers wanting to go home on the last bus. On these occasions the small 14-seaters were clearly inadequate.

The first mention of the Dobson sons as part of the business was when Middlesbrough Council licensed two 14-seat buses to John Dobson & Sons on 20th January 1925. Dobson himself will have been about 57 at this time.

One of the two buses licensed on that date was registered AJ 4610, a Maxwell new to Robinson's Motors Ltd of Scarborough, being licensed to them in July 1920 and August 1923. It was noted as a charabanc with Robinson's. No registration number was given for the other bus, which could well have been the Albion X 7953, perhaps on renewal and therefore familiar to the clerk. Another vehicle acquired by Dobson, probably later in 1925, was the Ford Model T registered PT 1410. This had a bus-lorry convertible body built by W G Edmond, and was photographed at the bodybuilder's in the spring of 1923 prior to registration. As new it was lettered for T H Southall of Stockton and named "Vera", with the wording "Parties catered for" on one side and "Haulage contractor" on the other, but was not licensed in Middlesbrough until December 1924, and then as a 14-seater for pleasure parties only. This vehicle did not feature in the town's licence renewals list the following September. It had probably passed to Dobson by then.

A new bus of AA manufacture, again a 14-seater, was licensed to John Dobson & Sons by Middlesbrough Council on 16th June 1925 after being deferred the previous month. This was registered DC 4276, and it would thus appear that 1925 saw the growth of the fleet to at least four buses, the others being X 7953, AJ 4610 and PT 1410. This makes it seem unlikely that the 1921 Ford convertible(s) DC 1109/89 were still owned.

Operation continued throughout 1926, with X 7953 noted in February to be operating without displaying the timetable and fare list. There were several further vehicle changes. The new AA bus was apparently not satisfactory, because in March 1926 its licence was transferred to a new Reo 14-seater registered PY 4691. In June a new Chevrolet PY 5202, yet again a 14-seater, was licensed to replace PT 1410, and another similar bus registered DC 6726 was licensed in December. During the year the bus station was brought into use at the Exchange, Middlesbrough on 16th July, and the Dobson's Lingdale departures were transferred to one of the stands. Early pictures of the bus station show PY 5202 on the stand.

In this period there was widespread rapid development of bus services, which caused increasing concern to Middlesbrough Council. A review in late 1926 was presented to the Watch Committee on 6th January 1927, from which we learn that Dobson's service to Lingdale via Ormesby, Guisborough, Charltons and Boosbeck ran every two hours, whilst the similar service provided by Cleveland Motor Services (note their revised title introduced in 1926) ran hourly. This, with very small

*The giant pneumatic tyre was featured on 1926 Reo **PY 4691** with Edmond body. It was photographed at the Lingdale terminus of the Middlesbrough service, with the mine winding gear in the background. (Edmond & Milburn Ltd)*

buses, does not seem much to us nowadays, especially as people did not then generally have cars, and we must remember that the operators' enthusiasm to expand was tempered by a climate of considerable economic hardship.

No doubt to match the competition, Dobson applied to increase his service to hourly, to depart Middlesbrough at 10 minutes past the hour. It was noted by the committee on 10th February 1927 that these buses, if approved, would be running 5 minutes in front of United as far as Guisborough on Saturdays only - the United service at that date ran Middlesbrough-Guisborough-Loftus-Whitby. Consideration was deferred, but appears to have been granted

subsequently. Further reviews of services were made by Middlesbrough Council and culminated the following year in the formation of a Regional Advisory Committee on Traffic Control. The revisions which were proposed to take effect on 23rd May 1927 would result in a combined ten-minute service between Middlesbrough and Guisborough, with Dobson's "Charltonian" on the hour, Cleveland Motor Services at 10 and 40 minutes past, United at 20 and 50, and Loftus Motor Service at 30 minutes past. This gives a vivid picture of the highly competitive situation in which Dobson was operating.

Yet another new make of vehicle joined the fleet during 1927, and with a larger capacity. This was DC 7328, a

*The iron ore mined in the Cleveland hills was bought and sold in the 1868 Exchange building in Middlesbrough, and a bus station was opened here in July 1926. Dobson's Chevrolet **PY 5202** of June 1926 is in the centre background of each picture. The upper view shows United's 1923 Daimler CB **B107** (**PW 128**) on service 35 to Whitby via Loftus and a 1921 Bristol of Middlesbrough Corporation. The lower view, heavily touched up, is a little later, with United Associated Daimler **E99** (**PW 8638**) of September 1926 and Middlesbrough Corporation's small Dennis **70** (**DC 7279**) new in April 1927. The prominence of United in these views was indeed prophetic. (Upper: Dickson & Benson Ltd/Courtesy Robin Cook. Lower: picture postcard)*

17

20-seat Laffly, licensed by Middlesbrough on 17th June 1927. The fleet at this time would have totalled at least four, viz. the Reo PY 4691, Chevrolets PY 5202 and DC 6726 and Laffly DC 7328. As already noted, PT 1410 and DC 4276 had gone, and the increased requirement of the hourly service has to be balanced against the possible withdrawal of X 7953 and AJ 4610 which would then have been quite old by the standards of the time. It is of course always possible that there were one or two other vehicles which remain unidentified.

The new Regional Advisory Committee on Traffic Control met on 7th February 1928, and among other things proposed standard running times for the various routes, with Guisborough to be 35 and Lingdale 55 minutes from Middlesbrough. Mr Jones of Cleveland Motor Services and Mr Dobson of Charltonian Bus Service attended, and Mr Jones contested some of the times, but the Committee recommended that they should be adopted as stated. It is interesting to observe that in 2003 the equivalent bus service, number 28, is still scheduled to take 55 minutes from Middlesbrough to Lingdale, although in the 1960s it was only 48 minutes.

10. Saltburn to Danby, 1928-29

Early in 1928, John Dobson had applied for a licence to Saltburn Council who arranged to inspect his bus on 28th February. Dobson's proposal was initially for a service from Saltburn to Lingdale, and subsequently for Saltburn-Lingdale-Danby, but the Council deferred his applications on 13th April and again on 12th November

1928 before refusing on 10th December.

There were already other operators on the route between Saltburn and Lingdale. Keith M Watson appears to have commenced in April 1927 and William Godsmark in February 1928. The latter applied in July 1928 to operate beyond Lingdale to Danby, and whilst the evidence of the council minutes is unclear, it is probable that he did so for a few months in the latter part of that year.

The Council's refusal of Dobson was based there being one operator (presumably Godsmark) already running to Danby and on the surprising figure of 46 buses a day to Lingdale. This would mean that over a 15-hour day Lingdale had an average of a bus every 20 minutes, which must have included journeys from Middlesbrough as well as from Saltburn. After making a further application and submitting his proposed timetable details, Dobson was granted a licence on 11th February 1929, to leave Saltburn for Lingdale, Castleton and Danby at 8.30am and 10.30am, then hourly until 10.30pm to Lingdale. In practice, at least by April the service was only two hourly.

An increase in Watson's Saltburn-Lingdale service from two-hourly to hourly had been licensed on 11th June 1928. The licence was transferred to the Cleveland Motor Service on 2nd October, probably meaning that the service had changed hands in the September. It further passed to the LNER-controlled Eastern Express Motors Ltd of West Hartlepool on 1st May 1929 and then to United (who numbered it 26) on 8th August 1929.

In the meantime an incursion of particular significance had taken place on Dobson's route between Saltburn and Danby. On 12th April 1929, Middlesbrough council licensed Smith's Safeway Services, based in the town, to operate thence to Marske, Skelton, Lingdale, Castleton and Danby, with departures at 15 and 45 minutes past the hour. It was noted, almost certainly in reference to John Dobson, that only a portion of the proposed route was covered hitherto, and this by a two-hourly service. Nevertheless, it seems extremely unlikely that Safeway intended to run to Danby every half hour, and a reference two months later in June suggests an hourly service with buses departing Middlesbrough at 35 minutes past the hour. By January 1930 the reference was to a two-hourly service departing at 45 minutes past the even hour, but wildly ambitious applications to increase the service continued to be made. They were refused, not only in January but also in March, June and July. Details show that the route between Skelton and Lingdale on this service was by the direct road, timed to take eight minutes instead of the fifteen minutes needed by John Dobson and others to cover the more populous route via Skelton Green and Boosbeck.

In May 1929 R A Barker of Skelton applied unsuccessfully to operate between Saltburn and Lingdale. Even after this, yet another Saltburn-Lingdale operator was L Thwaites of Redcar, who probably started in June 1929. This meant that there were now four operators on the section from Four Lane Ends through Skelton to Lingdale, which could not last even with at least one operator (Safeway) using the direct road as noted above.

*The GMC registered **DC 8551** and again with Edmond body was new in September 1928 and is seen with route board for the Saltburn-Danby service for which a licence was granted the following February. Note the "Charltonian" fleetname on the side. (Edmond & Milburn Ltd)*

*The Chevrolet **DC 9416** of May 1929 was photographed at Saltburn ready for a journey to Danby with Driver Bill Dobson and Conductor Mitchell. (Pam Wilson Collection via Freddie Dadd)*

Thwaites ceased on 6th January 1930, and the hourly United service (26) was discontinued without replacement from 8th January. In the meantime, William Godsmark, trading as "Alexandra", persevered on the route. It was noted by Saltburn Council on 7th January 1930 that the Charltonian service (Dobson) would depart for Lingdale at 20 minutes past each hour, and the Alexandra service (Godsmark) at 10 past each hour. This is likely to have been an intended increase from two-hourly to hourly for Dobson on the Saltburn-Lingdale section, in view of the withdrawal of Thwaites and United. If it ever took place, it was short-lived.

11. Struggling On, 1928-29

Whilst the development of the service between Saltburn and Danby could be seen as progress for John Dobson, it was in reality a desperate attempt to survive. There were no rich pickings to be had, but the effort was bravely made to keep the family employed and some sort of living flowing in.

The small lightweight buses of the period were usually very short-lived, and constant fleet replacement for an operator like Dobson was more of an urgent necessity than a long term policy of sound investment. Two new 16-seaters came in 1928, which were

Chevrolet DC 8078 licensed on 18th May and the similar GMC DC 8551 licensed on 14th September.

In 1929 a slightly larger GMC was PY 9500 with 20 seats, registered on 26th February, but a reversion to 14 seats came with DC 9416 licensed on 10th May. This was to prove the last bus acquired by John Dobson, as far as the records permit us to know.

On 12th April 1929, he was granted an extra early morning journey from Lingdale at 6.25am right through to the Transporter bridge at Middlesbrough, then leaving the Exchange stand for Lingdale at 8am. Also granted was a late evening run at 9.30pm from Danby through to Middlesbrough, and departing back to Lingdale at 10.50pm.

As with the Saltburn-Lingdale route, John Dobson's service from Middlesbrough to Lingdale was strongly contested. The Cleveland Motor Services was the senior competitor and indeed had begun regular operation six months before Dobson in 1924. By May 1927, as already noted, they were running two buses an hour to Dobson's one. The following month they were licensed to extend certain journeys beyond Lingdale via the moor road to Whitby. At the same time the United company was also licensed to operate via the moors to Whitby (presumably via Lingdale although not stated in known sources until 1929). This service ran through from Durham as service 15 but the Middlesbrough-Whitby section was withdrawn for the winter after September 1927 and similarly in 1928, in which year it had been renumbered 38. By contrast, the Cleveland Motor Service maintained a winter service with 3 or 4 journeys a day.

In theory a slight amelioration of the competition occurred on 13th April 1928 when the Cleveland Motor Service was licensed to run its Whitby journeys in and out of Middlesbrough via Marton and Nunthorpe Station, thus removing those workings from Dobson's section of route via Ormesby. In practice, as these were timed ten minutes behind Dobson's journeys, he would not have benefitted.

As noted already, the Cleveland Motor Services operation passed to Eastern Express on 1st May 1929, and then to United on 8th August. If John Dobson's previous two years of competition from the giant United with its summer-only through buses to Whitby was marginal, it was now a very different matter when the same company came to be the dominant operator on the local Middlesbrough - Lingdale service.

United absorbed the acquired workings from Middlesbrough to Lingdale and to Whitby into its existing service 38. Hitherto this had operated via Ormesby, but from 8th August 1929 the expanded service also incorporated the Eastern Express (ex-Cleveland Motor Service) journeys via Marton. In a comprehensive revision, United re-routed the whole of its Middlesbrough-Lingdale-Whitby service via Marton from 18th September 1929, leaving to Dobson the Lingdale passengers on the route via Ormesby. This was of minimal benefit, because United had a strong presence on the Ormesby route with other services.

Towards the end of 1929, Dobson applied on 22nd November to increase his Saturday frequency between Middlesbrough and Lingdale, but it was refused.

*Safeway's similar Chevrolet **CN 4086** was working the Middlesbrough-Marske-Lingdale-Danby service as stated on the side route board when it was involved in an accident, probably in 1929, making the "Safeway" name seem somewhat inappropriate. The service covered most of Dobson's route. (Press cutting)*

12. John Dobson Sells Out - 1930

Although the business was repeatedly referred to as John Dobson & Sons in the period from 1925, when it was disposed of in the year 1930 the arrangements referred only to John Dobson himself. Dobson would be 63 in 1930 and his business must have been failing, if we are to judge by what he received from the sale. His first proposal was to sell to Mr T Coatsworth of Buittle Place, Lingdale, and on 4th April 1930 Middlesbrough Council was willing for the licences to be transferred provided that two of the present buses were

renovated, a new 30-seater was put on the road without delay, and a second new 30-seater was brought into use by 1st October 1930. These requirements suggest that Dobson's fleet was falling into decay, and that he was having to run extras (causing additional congestion in the town) which would not have been necessary if he had had larger buses.

When the Committee met on 16th May it heard that Mr Coatsworth had not proceeded with the proposed purchase. Doubtless he too was not in a position to invest in two 30-seaters. Instead, John Dobson had sold the business to Smith's Safeway Services and at Middlesbrough the licences had been transferred temporarily on 12th April. In Saltburn, the transfer of licences from Dobson to Safeway was considered on 4th June and granted on 7th July, Safeway having been asked to operate more punctually and to provide better vehicles. By this time they had in any case already been in possession of the service for several weeks.

The formal agreement was made on 12th April 1930, when John Dobson sold his rights in the services to Smith's Safeway Services Ltd. There were five vehicles included in the sale, listed as PY 9500 (GMC 20 seats), DC 6726, DC 8078 and DC 9146 (error for 9416) (Chevrolet 14 seats) and DC 8551 (GMC 14 seats). The terms included the usual agreement to relinquish the existing licences in favour of the purchaser, and the price paid was £790. A second agreement made on the same date shows the tight corner in which Dobson found himself at a time when he should have been reaping the fruits of his life's work. He accepted to buy back the five vehicles within fourteen days for £400. This appears to mean that he had only £390 with which to settle any outstanding debts including hire purchase, and in effect a two-week loan of a further £400. The record of these agreements survives in the United archive in the Durham County Record Office (File D/UAS 704, Smith's Safeway Services). The sale did not involve any premises, but the buildings shown in the early photographs at the Slapewath side of Charltons were later the sheds where the buses were kept. After the war they were used by a blacksmith by the name of Russell. Buses PY 4691 and PY 5202, already withdrawn by 1930, had no other

recorded owners, while PY 9500 survived for a while as a lorry with Dobson, as noted below. There is no other record of how he disposed of the vehicles, except that one of them became a hen hut at Farndale's Tidkinhow farm at the foot of Birk Brow. There it remained slowly decaying until in the 1960s it was noticed that the roof had not rusted. An enterprising metals dealer realised it was aluminium and promptly removed it for scrap.

13. The Safeway Saga, 1930 to 1932

The Safeway business operated by James Smith and David Wilson Smith of Middlesbrough since 1927 was incorporated on 30th January 1930 as a limited company named Smith's Safeway Services Ltd. As we have seen, their operation from Middlesbrough to Danby had been licensed on 12th April 1929. Two Chevrolet 14-seaters, CN 4086/7, entered service on 16th August 1929 and were licensed by Middlesbrough Council for this route only. From 7th March 1930 an additional Safeway vehicle now similarly restricted was PY 7510, a secondhand small Dennis which had been acquired in 1927 after being new to Keith Watson earlier that year.

As we have also seen, the Safeway company purchased John Dobson's Charltonian bus service on 12th April 1930, with the Middlesbrough-Lingdale and Saltburn-Danby services but no premises. The Safeway timetables of 1930 showed notable development of early morning and late night journeys, at least partly to accommodate operation from their

Safeway Services, T

Stockton, Middlesbrough, South Bank, Grangetown, Redcar, Marske and Saltburn.

ROUTE IN MIDDLESBROUGH.
Middlesbrough, Exchange Bus Stand, Albert Road, Borough Road, Linthorpe Road, The Avenue, Cambridge Road.
Acklam Road, Thornaby via. Lane House Road.

	a.m.	a.m.	a.m.	a.m.	a.m.	a.m.	p.m.	p.m.	p.m.	p.m.	p.m.
STOCKTON (Yarm Lane Corner)						7-15		10-15	10-45	11-15	11-45
Lane House Road (Pass about)						7-20		10-20	10-50	11-20	11-50
Kirby Schools (Pass about)						7-30		10-30	11-0	11-30	12-0
Middlesbro' Exchange Bus Stand	5-15	5-45	6-15	6-45	7-15	7-45	Then every half-hour until	10-45	11-15	11-45	12-15
South Bank Bennett's Corner	5-30	6-0	6-30	7-0	7-30	8-0		11-0	11-30	12-0	
Grangetown	5-35	6-5	6-35	7-5	7-35	8-5		11-5	11-35	12-5	
Dormanstown Crossing	5-40	6-10	6-40	7-10	7-40	8-10		11-10	11-40	12-10	
Redcar (Swan Hotel)	5-45	6-15	6-45	7-15	7-45	8-15		11-15	11-45	12-15	
Marske		6-25	6-55	7-25	7-55	8-25		11-25			
SALTBURN		6-45	7-15	7-45	8-15	8-45		11-45			
SALTBURN					6-45		10-15				
Marske					6-55		10-25				
Redcar (Zetland Park)	5-5	5-35	6-5	6-35	7-5		10-35	11-5	11-35	12-5	
Dormanstown Crossing	5-15	5-45	6-15	6-45	7-15		10-45	11-15	11-45	12-15	
Grangetown	5-25	5-55	6-25	6-55	7-25		10-55	11-25	11-55	12-25	
South Bank	5-30	6-0	6-30	7-0	7-30	Then every half-hour until	11-0	11-30	12-0	12-30	
Middlesbrough Bus Stand	5-45	6-15	6-45	7-15	7-45		11-15	11-45	12-15	12-45	
Kirby Schools			6-55	7-25	7-55		11-25				
Thornaby (Lane House Road)			7-5	7-35	8-5		11-35				
STOCKTON			7-10	7-40	8-10		11-40				

SUNDAYS.—First Bus leaves Stockton 9-15 a.m. and Middlesbrough 9-45 a.m. for Redcar. First Bus leaves Saltburn 10-45 a.m. and Redcar 11-5 a.m for Middlesbrough and Stockton. Then as Week-days.

Middlesbrough to Castleton & Danby

via. South Bank, Grangetown, Eston, Marske, Skelton, Lingdale and Over the Moors.

	a.m.	p.m.	p.m.
MIDDLESBROUGH	6-45	8-45	10-45
South Bank	6-57	8-57	10-57
Grangetown Bridge	7-2	9-2	11-2
Newtown	7-6	9-6	11-6
Eston	7-8	9-8	11-8
Lazenby	7-13	9-13	
Kirkleatham	7-19	9-19	
Marske	7-27	9-27	
Skelton	7-42	9-42	
Lingdale	7-50	9-50	
Commondale (Lane Ends)	8-0	10-0	
Castleton	8-14	10-14	
DANBY	8-25	10-25	
DANBY	8-30	10-30	
Castleton	8-41	10-41	
Commondale (Lane Ends)	8-50	10-50	
Lingdale	9-5	11-5	
Skelton	9-13	11-13	
Marske	9-28	11-28	
Kirkleatham	9-36	11-36	
Lazenby	9-42	11-42	
Eston	9-47	11-47	11-10
Newton	9-50	11-50	11-14
Grangetown	9-53	11-53	11-16
South Bank	9-58	11-58	11-21
MIDDLESBROUGH	10-10	12-10	11-33

(Then every two hours until)

SUNDAYS—First Bus leaves Middlesbro' 8-45 a.m. then as Weekdays. First Bus leaves Danby 10-30 a.m. then as Weekdays.

ALWAYS TRAVEL SAFEWAY and SUPPORT

24

'ime Tables.

Saltburn, Skelton, Lingdale, Castleton & Danby

	a.m.	a.m		p.m.
SALTBURN (Stn. Square)	6-30	8-30		10-30
Skelton Institute	6-40	8-40		10-40
Skelton Green	6-45	8-45	Then every two hours until	10-45
Boosbeck	6-50	8-50		10-50
Lingdale	6-55	8-55		10-55
Lockwood Beck	7-0	9-0		
Commondale (White Cross)	7-5	9-5		
Castleton	7-19	9-19		
DANBY	7-30	9-30		

DANBY	7-30	9-30		9-30
Castleton	7-41	9-41		9-41
Commondale (White Cross)	7-55	9-55	Then every two hours until	9-55
Lockwood Beck	8-0	10-0		10-0
Lingdale	8-5	10-5		10-5
Boosbeck	8-10	10-10		10-10
Skelton Green	8-15	10-15		10-15
Skelton Institute	8-20	10-20		10-20
SALTBURN (Stn. Square)	8-30	10-30		10-30

SUNDAYS—First Bus leaves Saltburn 10-30 a.m., then as Weekdays. First Bus leaves Danby 11-30 a.m,, then as Weekdays.

Passengers Change at Lingdale for Charltons, Guisbrough and Old Ormesby.

Middlesbrough, Guisborough, Charltons, Boosbeck, Lingdale.

	a.m.	a.m.	a.m.	a.m.		p.m.	p.m.
MIDDLESBRO'	5-0	7-0	8-0	9-0		10-50	
Red Lion Ormesby	5-15	7-15	8-15	9-15	Then every hour until	11-5	
Guisborough	5-30	7-35	8-35	9-35		11-25	
Charltons	5-40	7-45	8-45	9-45		11-35	
Boosbeck	5-45	7-50	8-50	9-50		11-40	
LINGDALE	5-50	7-55	8-55	9-55		11-45·	

LINGDALE	6-7	8-7	9-7	10-7?		10-0	11-45
Boosbeck	6-12	8-12	9-12	10-12		10-5	11-50
Charltons	6-17	8-17	9-17	10-17	Then every hour until	10-10	12-55
Guisborough	6-25	8-25	9-25	10-25		10-18	12-5
Red Lion Ormesby	6-45	8-45	9-45	10-45		10-38	12-20
MIDDLESBRO'	6-57	8-57	9-57	10-57		10-50	12-32

SUNDAYS—First bus leaves Middlesbrough 10 a.m. then as Weekdays
First bus leaves Lingdale 11-7 a.m. then as Week-days

Passengers change at Lingdale for Lockwood Beck, Castleton & Danby Connection every hour.

PRIVATE ENTERPRISE !

The earliest known published timetables for the services operated by John Dobson's "Charltonian" are in fact those produced by his successor, Smith's Safeway Services Ltd. The tables shown here are arranged as a display poster rather than as a booklet or handbill. They were current during 1930, from April when the company purchased the Dobson business, until November when it abandoned its Middlesbrough-Marske-Danby service. Various changes had been required in order to run the buses from the Middlesbrough depot instead of from Charltons, as discussed in the text. (Omnibus Society Collection/Courtesy John Bennett)

main depot in North Ormesby Road, Middlesbrough. It is possible that the Saltburn-Danby service was operated from premises in Redcar.

The former Charltonian service continued to run on the hour from Middlesbrough to Lingdale. Departures from Saltburn to Danby were at 30 minutes past the even hour, suggesting that the original timetable of February 1929 had perhaps never been changed. Safeway's own Middlesbrough-Marske-Danby service also continued at 45 minutes past the even hour, thereby retaining the overall hourly coverage between Lingdale and Danby. However, the injunction to passengers to make connections at Lingdale collapsed for anyone going from Guisborough to Danby at 35 minutes past the odd hour, because that particular connection was missed by five minutes.

Following their acquisition of John Dobson's business, nine vehicles were licensed by Saltburn Council to Safeway in July 1930. They probably included the small buses restricted by Middlesbrough Council to the Danby service. At about the time of the takeover, buses were running via Ainthorpe on the Castleton-Danby section, owing to the state of the road on the direct route. Middlesbrough Council, rather pompously it seems, insisted at first that the original route must be followed, but later recorded (presumably with approval) that the Ainthorpe route was being used with effect from 14th August.

During that summer Safeway made several applications to increase their Middlesbrough-Marske-Danby service from every two hours to every half hour - quite a prospect for such rural territory - and there was also an application to increase the Middlesbrough-Guisborough-Lingdale service from hourly to half-hourly. Further, several applications were made for a Scarborough service via Lingdale. All were refused.

The whole share capital of Smith's Safeway Services Ltd was purchased by nominees of United Automobile Services Ltd in October 1930. The use of nominees served to hide United's involvement at this stage, and Safeway was to all appearances unchanged. In fact United reorganized the financial state of the undertaking, sending a number of buses back to the hire purchase companies, increasing fares, and reducing services which competed needlessly with their own. One such service was Middlesbrough-Marske-Lingdale-Danby which, far from being increased fourfold to half-hourly, was withdrawn altogether on Saturday 22nd November 1930. It was stated that Middlesbrough passengers would still be able to reach Danby by changing at Lingdale on to Safeway's Saltburn-Lingdale-Danby service which was running every two hours.

On 16th January 1931 Middlesbrough Council approved the withdrawal of Safeway's hourly Middlesbrough-Lingdale service, which was of course the former Dobson operation, presumably still running via Ormesby. United was permitted consequently to retime their Middlesbrough-Lingdale service to give (with the Middlesbrough-Loftus service) a regular 15-minute frequency to Guisborough. It was also noted that United would take over Safeway's service between Saltburn, Lingdale and Danby, retaining the connection at

UNITED

Service 26

SALTBURN - LINGDALE - DANBY

Commencing on FRIDAY, 17th JULY, 1931.

THE FOLLOWING

REVISED SERVICE

WILL BE IN OPERATION :—

	a.m. N.S.	a.m.	p.m.		p.m.	p.m.
SALTBURN (Station Sq.) depart	8 35	10 35	12 35		8 35	10 35
SKELTON (Institute) pass about	8 45	10 45	12 45		8 45	10 45
SKELTON GREEN „	8 50	10 50	12 50	Then	8 50	—
BOOSBECK „	8 55	10 55	12 55	every	8 55	—
LINGDALE „	9 0	11 0	1 0	TWO	9 0	—
LOCKWOOD BECK „	9 5	11 5	1 5	Hours	9 5	—
COMMONDALE (White Cross) „	9 10	11 10	1 10	until	9 10	—
CASTLETON „	9 24	11 24	1 24		9 24	—
DANBY arrive	9 35	11 35	1 35		9 35	—

	N.S.	N.S.	a.m.			
DANBY depart	7 35	9 35	11 35		7 35	9 35
CASTLETON pass about	7 46	9 46	11 46		7 46	9 46
COMMONDALE (White Cross) „	8 0	10 0	12 0	Then	8 0	10 0
LOCKWOOD BECK „	8 5	10 5	12 5	every	8 5	10 5
LINGDALE „	8 10	10 10	12 10	TWO	8 10	10 10
BOOSBECK „	8 15	10 15	12 15	Hours	8 15	10 15
SKELTON GREEN „	8 20	10 20	12 20	until	8 20	10 20
SKELTON INSTITUTE „	8 25	10 25	12 25		8 25	10 25
SALTBURN (Station Sq.) arrive	8 35	10 35	12 35		8 35	10 35

N.S., Not Sundays.

TEES-SIDE DISTRICT OFFICE :—23 WILSON STREET, MIDDLESBROUGH.
('Phone 3227.)

500. Jordison & Co., Ltd., Printers, Middlesbrough.

The number 26 reappeared for the former Safeway and Charltonian Saltburn to Danby service when it passed to United on 1st February 1931. The handbill announcing the change is not known to have survived, but this revised version of 17th July is understood to be little different.(United)

Lingdale for Middlesbrough-Danby passengers. At the same time, by a revision of service 33 (Redcar-Lingdale) United was to offer a more regular frequency between Lingdale, Skelton and Four Lane Ends.

These revisions took place on 1st February 1931, with the whole of the former Charltonian service thus being absorbed into United's network from this date. The rationalisation whereby Safeway's ex-Dobson timings between Middlesbrough and Lingdale had been withdrawn meant that strictly speaking the Dobson service no longer had a direct successor, particularly in respect of the section via Ormesby, but it is nearer the truth to recognise that the sequence of business purchases meant that the Dobson mantle had passed to United. The reduced Safeway undertaking ran until 30th November 1932, after which the remaining services were transferred to United and the company wound up.

Under United, the ex-Charltonian Middlesbrough-Lingdale service was part of the revised 38 service, and the number 26 was resurrected for the Saltburn-Lingdale-Danby service. For a brief period, on (or by) 1st March 1932 the number 26 was changed to 23, but a grand scheme of revised service numbers affecting the whole United network followed on 1st June. For the time being, it made little difference when the bus itself was not equipped to display a number, as can be seen in the accompanying picture of conductress Bertha Stubbs. However, in the 1932 scheme Middlesbrough-Lingdale became 58 and Saltburn-Danby was 86, and these numbers eventually became familiar to generations of passengers, although circa 1945 the Lingdale-Danby section became part of service 89 to and from Middlesbrough. These became 258, 277 and 259 in the next big scheme on 16th June 1968. Nowadays the successors are Arriva North East services 28/28A and 48/49, where we can recall John Dobson's pioneering work as we ride through Charltons and other local villages on today's giant-sized buses.

14. Survivors

There were two notable survivors after United had, by 1932, conquered all its other competitors in the East Cleveland district. One, William Godsmark, continued to operate his "Alexandra" bus service between Saltburn and Lingdale until he sold out to United as from 9th May 1937. His journeys were absorbed into the existing 86 service which was increased to hourly between Saltburn and Lingdale, with Danby served as before. Godsmark's two buses were included in the purchase but not operated by United. The other survivor was J C Pickering, one of the partners in the erstwhile Cleveland Motor Service. He formed Saltburn Motor Services and operated various local routes until he sold out to Cleveland Transit on 1st August 1974.

15. To Conclude

Council minutes record many instances of bus operators failing to reach the authority's requirements, flouting them, or causing constant aggravation. No doubt the operators in turn perceived the council as harassing them. John Dobson does not feature in any such contention, nor is he ever censured except indirectly at the end

The small legal ownership lettering at the right identifies a vehicle of William Godsmark's "Alexandra" bus service, which competed with John Dobson's "Charltonian" between Lingdale and Saltburn, where the picture was probably taken. The picture was discovered in the archives of John Dobson's daughter Annie (Mrs. Nunn), so there is some probability that the conductor was her brother Walter, who was born in 1914. Here, maybe aged 16 or 17, he had perhaps just joined Godsmark after the 1930 demise of his father's business? Otherwise nothing is known of the crew or the vehicle. (Dobson Collection)

(when he was probably in dire straits) when improvements were required of his successors. This is to his credit, although it probably also means that he was not as pushy or ruthless as his competitors, who succeeded in running him off the road. He was perhaps a true gentleman.

He was also a man of vision, even though the business side of things was not altogether his cup of tea. Like so many with an affliction or disability he strove to better himself. Yet it was inevitable that with so much competition continually developing he would struggle to survive.

The recording of change of use in the registration of one of the buses suggests that after the sale of his bus business John Dobson worked for a while in goods transport from a base in Middlesbrough. The GMC bus PY 9500 had become a 2-ton goods vehicle by April 1931, licensed to J Dobson, North Ormesby. It was last licensed to 30th June 1932, when he would have been 65. We do not know how much longer he might have continued to work. John Dobson died at 41 Margrove Park in 1945, aged 78.

As for the sons, from about 1932 to 1936 my father Bill Dobson (born

1906) lived at Margrove Park, where he kept a lorry in a large corrugated iron shed, possibly after taking over from his father. It is understood that both he and his brother Albert worked for United for a while, and I remember his PSV driver's badge. Albert then left the area to work for Leicester Corporation as a bus driver until he retired in the mid 1960s, whilst Bill became a driver for Smith's Transport of Middlesbrough, perhaps until about 1942. This was none other than James Smith who had been the prime mover of Smith's Safeway Services Ltd, so in effect Bill came back to the man who had purchased his father's business, a contact which was probably his route to the job in those depression years. Smith had reacquired the Safeway depot in North Ormesby Road, Middlesbrough in 1931-32 when, under United control, the limited company had disposed of it. His haulage company was recorded under several slightly different names, though there might not be any significance in this. After other lorry driving jobs Bill became a fish and chip shop proprietor in Guisborough until shortly before his death in 1969.

Walter got a job as a driver on London Transport and stayed until retirement age. The Dobson in-laws Wilf and Alf Smith who, as noted, were drivers for Charltonian subsequently transferred to the United depot at Middlesbrough. Alf also had a smallholding on the so-called Wilderness road out of Middlesbrough almost opposite the greyhound track. He died some twelve years ago aged about 90 and one of my last conversations with him was about Tommy Longstaff, who was chief engineer at the Middlesbrough depot and had worked previously at West Hartlepool. As for Wilf, he became chargehand cleaner at the Loftus United depot after the war, and his daughter Doreen became a conductress there. Her second husband was Bob Senior, a United driver also at Loftus. Other names which come to mind as drivers for Charltonian are "King" Sanderson, "Rattler" Morgan, and (I think) Alderson and Suckling.

In the next generation I worked for the gas industry for forty years. Albert's son Peter founded and is now chairman of Sidetracker fork lift trucks in the Midlands and his son David (great grandson of John Dobson) is Managing Director, so the spirit of enterprise lives on in the family.

The invaluable help of Freddie Dadd of Guisborough (formerly of Charltons) and his diligence and interest in all things Charltonian have resulted in the procurement of many of the photographs which enhance this booklet, and I owe him a particular debt. Some of his photographs had in turn been provided by Pam Wilson, author of the recent book *Around Guisborough* (Tempus Publishing, Stroud, 2003, ISBN 0 7524 3075 0, 128pp, £12.99). The photographic archive of Patricia Pearson has also been of much interest and help. Local historian and publisher Peter Tuffs has provided some helpful background regarding the history of the local ironstone mining, and his book catalogue indicates the wealth of research which this subject has attracted. I am further indebted to the Omnibus Society, to its members John D Watson and Philip Battersby for archive research, to the staffs of Teesside Archives Department and the

Durham and North Yorkshire County Record Offices who have assisted them, and to John Banks for technical expertise in bringing the book to publication. Significant information has also been gleaned from the United timetables and leaflets of the period, some of which have been made available by Arriva North East Ltd.

Front cover illustrations: John Dobson's two routes shared the one mile between Boosbeck and Lingdale. The small picture shows his Reo bus **PY 4691** waiting at Lingdale before leaving for Middlesbrough. In a scene some forty years later, the large picture shows a Bristol MW6G of United Automobile Services, **2677** (**8677 HN**), climbing Cherry Tree Bank out of Boosbeck on the service from Saltburn on 6th August 1969. *(John Banks)*

*The conductress seen here at Danby circa 1932 was Bertha Stubbs, who had started with United at Redcar depot in 1924. The bus was United's Leyland **AM130** (**TY 5609**) on the former Charltonian service from Saltburn. (Courtesy Brenda Norris)*

Registr'n Number	Chassis	Body	Seats	Date New[1]	Date Acq'd	Date Sold
AJ443	De Dion Bouton 8hp		car		by 1911[2]	Note[3]
DC337	Napier		Ch	6/12	6/13	9/20[4]
J2611	Thornycroft		Ch22?	-/14		
DC1109[5]	Ford T		convertible 14	c.1920	by 5/21	
X7953	Albion	Edmond	B14?F	1919[6]	-/23	c.1927
AJ4610	Maxwell		Ch14	7/20	by 1/25[7]	c.1927
DC4276	AA		14	5/25	5/25	3/26
PT1410	Ford T	Edmond	convertible 14	-/23	c. 1925[8]	6/26
PY4691	Reo	"	B14F	2/26	2/26	3/29[9]
PY5202	Chevrolet	"	"	6/26	6/26	Note[10]
DC6726	"		14	12/26	12/26	4/30[11]
DC7328	Laffly		20	6/27	6/27	
DC8078	Chevrolet		16[12]	5/28	5/28	4/30
DC8551	GMC	Edmond	B16F[13]	9/28	9/28	"
PY9500	"		20	2/29	2/29	" [14]
DC9416	Chevrolet		B14F	5/29	5/29	"

1 - Most of the dates shown are taken from Council minutes and refer to licensing. Dates of actual manufacture, registration, purchase or sale could be slightly different.

2 - Purchased from Dr W W Stainthorpe, Guisborough, date variously given as by 1909 or 1911.

3 - Registration number re-issued 26/1/21 to a motor-cycle.

4 - Registered as a lorry with new owner, unidentified.

5 - A Middlesbrough licence was sought for DC 1109 in 5/21 and for DC 1189 in 7/21. As discussed in the text, these are assumed to refer to the same vehicle, with one of DC 1109 or DC 1189 as an error for the other.

6 - The registration number dates from 1919 and the body from 1923 as discussed in the text. It is assumed that the complete vehicle was supplied by Edmond to Dobson in 1923.

7 - AJ 4610 was licensed in 7/20 and 8/23 as a 14-seat charabanc to Robinson's Motors Ltd, Scarborough, from whom it was purchased by Dobson. Middlesbrough Council noted it as a 14-seat bus in his application of 1/25. He perhaps operated the vehicle as a charabanc in 1924 and fitted a bus body later. To L Brown, Stockton, as lorry, last licensed 6/28.

8 - Bought from T H Southall, 11 Carr Street, Oxbridge, Stockton, who had owned it from new.

9 - No other recorded owners. Registered void 12/30.

10 - Gone by 4/30. No other recorded owners. Registered void 12/30.

11 - Vehicles shown as withdrawn in 4/30 were sold to Smith's Safeway Services Ltd with the business and were then repurchased for disposal.

12, 13 - Listed in the sale agreement (12/4/30) as a 14-seater.

14 - Recorded as 2½-ton goods with J Dobson, North Ormesby, 17/4/31. Last licensed 6/32.